Bookkeeping

Learning The Simple And Effective Methods of Effective Methods Of Bookkeeping

(Easy Way To Master The Art Of Bookkeeping)

Jefferey Traylor

Published By **Jackson Denver**

Jefferey Traylor

All Rights Reserved

Bookkeeping: Learning The Simple And Effective Methods of Effective Methods Of Bookkeeping (Easy Way To Master The Art Of Bookkeeping)

ISBN   978-1-7388267-5-9

No part of this guidebook shall be reproduced in any form without permission in writing from the publisher except in the case of brief quotations embodied in critical articles or reviews.

Legal & Disclaimer

The information contained in this ebook is not designed to replace or take the place of any form of medicine or professional medical advice. The information in this ebook has been provided for educational & entertainment purposes only.

The information contained in this book has been compiled from sources deemed reliable, and it is accurate to the best of the Author's knowledge; however, the Author cannot guarantee its accuracy and validity and cannot be held liable for any errors or omissions. Changes are periodically made to this book. You must consult your doctor or get professional medical advice before using any of the suggested remedies, techniques, or information in this book.

Upon using the information contained in this book, you agree to hold harmless the Author from and against any damages, costs, and expenses, including any legal fees potentially resulting from the application of any of the information provided by this guide. This disclaimer applies to any damages or injury caused by the use and application, whether directly or indirectly, of any advice or information presented, whether for breach of contract, tort, negligence, personal injury, criminal intent, or under any other cause of action.

You agree to accept all risks of using the information presented inside this book. You need to consult a professional medical practitioner in order to ensure you are both able and healthy enough to participate in this program.

Table Of Contents

Chapter 1: Bookkeeping Principles And Fundamental Differences

If you're like most human beings, you possibly think of the words "debit" and "credit score" in phrases of the type of card you operate to pay for items when you buy groceries. When you use your debit card, the money comes immediately from your checking account; however while you operate your credit card, in place of money being deducted out of your financial institution account, the quantity of the purchase is added to the entire bill you'll pay your credit score card organization on the end of the month.

This is a totally primary know-how of debits and credits allow you to navigate the terminology of this part of recording monetary transactions on your business. However, within the global of bookkeeping, this critical concept is quite extra complex.

First, earlier than we discover the specifics of the way debits and credit are used to document transactions in bookkeeping, allow's keep in mind the fundamental equation upon which all accounting is primarily based:

Assets = Liabilities + Equity

Whenever you see a mathematical equation, you recognize that the 2 factors on either facet of the equals sign should have the same numeric cost, so the subsequent equations are accurate:

$2 + 1 + 1 = 4$

$3 + 1 = 4$

But this equation is wrong:

$2 + three = 4$

Because the price of a commercial enterprise is calculated the use of the accounting equation, Assets = Liabilities + Equity, the numeric values of these phrases need to be a balanced equation. If they're now not, then your commercial enterprise's books are out of stability, and on the way to create accurate financial statements, you'll ought to find in which you have got made bookkeeping errors.

Next, earlier than we study debits and credit in detail, we have to take a moment to recognize the phrases inside the accounting equation.

• Assets are any assets that your company owns that represent a destiny fee and may be expressed in financial cost. Cash is one form of asset, but there are many others. For example, investments, stock, actual estate, workplace supplies, gadget, and bills receivable, all represent resources that you own and that can be assigned a monetary fee. In addition, so-called "intangible assets" encompass your organization's recognition, your purchaser base, the perceived fee of your brand, and so forth.

● Liabilities are the quantity of extraordinary financial duties owed by way of your organization. So, your organization's liabilities may additionally include the ultimate stability on any mortgages, gadget leases, or commercial enterprise loans; accounts payable; or quantities acquired for destiny income which have not but been delivered.

● Equity is the amount of economic interest all of a employer's shareholders have in the agency. For example, in case you purchase 1,000 stocks of inventory in a new startup employer at $2.25 according to percentage, you can in my opinion declare $2,250.00 of that organisation's value as yours.

So, the accounting equation, Assets = Liabilities + Equity, manner that in order on your organization's books to be taken into consideration balanced and so as, you have to have the ability to reveal that the total price of all of your property is exactly equal to the overall price of all your liabilities plus the overall value of all of the equity all shareholders may also have on your business enterprise.

This seems like a daunting assignment, and that's why accounting uses both debits and credits to file transactions.

Importance of Debit and Credit Accounting

We began this chapter by means of considering a common knowledge of debits and credits – the use of your debit card takes money out of your checking account; using a credit score card adds money for your credit score card invoice. This is a outstanding start to knowledge the significance of the use of debits and credit to preserve correct books, but in phrases of bookkeeping, this concept is greater complex.

First, take into account the definition of belongings above. There are many sorts of property, starting from the stability in your business's predominant checking account, to the full value of your stock, to the value of your supplies and device, to the value of all the sales you've got made for that you are looking ahead to fee. As a result, an accurate bookkeeping system will need greater than just one account to track property.

Next, you could also have many forms of liabilities, consisting of money owed payable and future income, so you may also have more than one account to file all of your liabilities.

Finally, similarly to assets, liabilities, and fairness, your bookkeeping gadget will have to maintain track of sales, fees, profits, and losses.

Taken collectively, these categories of economic accounts — belongings, liabilities, equity, revenue, expenses, profits, and losses – comprise what accountants name the chart of bills and relying on the dimensions and complexity of your corporation, the chart of debts can turn out to be fairly complex.

One greater step, and the significance of debits and credits turns into clean. Returning to the authentic example of purchasing at your neighborhood department store, bear in mind what happens when you purchase some thing together with your debit card – the quantity of cash to your checking account is decreased, but the amount of cash in the department keep's checking account is expanded. In addition, even though you have got less cash after making the acquisition with the debit card, you have got multiplied the cost of your assets by using the price of the term to procure; and in return, the value of the shop's stock has decreased by means of the fee of the time they sold. The difference in making the purchase with a credit score card is that instead of lowering the quantity of cash to your checking account, you growth the amount of money you owe; further, the store does now not acquire an growth in the quantity of cash of their bank account, but they do see an boom inside the value of their bills receivable.

Thus, the concept in the back of debits and credits is that each single transaction has components – money is taken from one account, and money is added to any other account. Because a organization's books account for a potentially complicated chart of accounts, a gadget of debits and credit lets in the bookkeeper to report all transactions correctly and constantly.

Recording Debit and Credit in an Account

Figure three: Free Image

First, consider that during accounting, debit is abbreviated dr. And credit is abbreviated cr. Second, although it is not unusual to associate debit with deducting money and credit score with adding money, debits and credit in bookkeeping are used in a different way. Depending on which sort of transaction the agency engages in and which type of account is affected, debits and credit might also either increase or decrease the fee of any given account. Specifically:

- For asset bills (e.G., your employer's bank account):

o A debit will boom the value of the account; a credit score will decrease the fee of the account.

- For legal responsibility money owed (e.G., your accounts payable account):

o A debit will decrease the value of the account; a credit score will growth the price of the account.

- For equity money owed (e.G., the stocks an investor holds in your enterprise):

o A debit will decrease the cost of the account; a credit will growth the fee of the account.

This appears to be the opposite order of the manner you may normally consider debits and credit because it's miles based totally on the accounting equation, Assets = Liabilities + Equity. Thus, you can't boom your property unless you also growth your liabilities or fairness. As a result, debits and credits inside a bookkeeping device characteristic otherwise than in a simple take a look at check in.

Of direction, in some cases, recording a balanced transaction can also require growing the price of one asset account while reducing the fee of every other asset account (rather than a legal responsibility or equity account). In these instances, there are additional rules that govern the function of debits and credits:

- For revenue money owed:

o   A debit decreases the balance and a credit score increases the balance.

- For fee bills:

o   A debit will growth the balance and a credit score will decrease the balance.

- For gain money owed:

o   A debit decreases the balance and a credit will increase the balance.

- For loss bills:

o   A debit will growth the stability and a credit score will lower the stability.

Regardless, in terms of an real e book of accounts, debits are transaction values which might be entered on the left facet of an account, and credit are transaction values which can be entered at the right aspect of an account.

Third, for each unmarried transaction in bookkeeping, the entire amount recorded as a debit need to be offset via the exact same amount recorded as credit score. If the 2 aspects of the transaction are unequal, the books will now not balance, and the bookkeeping gadget will no longer receive the entry.

Let's look at some specific examples to clarify the concepts above.

For the first example, allow's expect your organisation sells computer add-ons. One of your customers purchases a video digicam attachment for a pc laptop at a value of $375.00. The sale results in an growth inside the value of your cash account. It additionally method which you have increased your revenue by means of changing stock into cash. To file this transaction using debits and credit, the bookkeeper will use two accounts: coins and sales. When you offered the digital camera attachment to the patron, you obtained $375.00 in cash, so the cash account is debited for 375. To document the associated boom in revenue, the bookkeeper credit the revenue account for the same quantity – 375.

Account	Debit	Credit
Cash	375	
Revenue		375

Alternatively, the information may be displayed as follows:

Cash

Debits	Credits
375	

Revenue

Debits   Credits

     375

In the subsequent example, allow's assume that your employer needs 10 new servers, and every server fees $1,000. You don't want to use your coins account to make this purchase, so you train your purchasing agent to shop for them on credit. The buy results in an boom to the fee of your fixed property account. Because they were purchased on credit score, there may be an identical boom to the cost of your accounts payable. Here is how the bookkeeper will report the transaction:

Account   Debit   Credit

Fixed Assets   10,000

Accounts Payable   10,000

Again, the same relationship may be displayed as follows:

Fixed Assets

Debits	Credits
375	

Accounts Payable

Debits	Credits
	375

Finally, right here are some additional recommendations to assist get you oriented to the sector of debits and credit:

Debit-Credit Table

Account Type	Increase	Decrease
Assets	Debit	Credit

Expenses	Debit	Credit
Liabilities	Credit	Debit
Equity	Credit	Debit
Revenue	Credit	Debit

Debit-Credit Acronyms

The following styles of debts (DEAL) are elevated with a debit:

- Dividends

- Expenses

- Assets

- Losses

The following styles of money owed (GIRLS) are expanded with a credit score:

- Gains

- Income

- Revenues

- Liabilities

- Stockholders' Equity

Debit-Credit Rules

Recording a debit approach:

- Increasing the value of an asset account

- Increasing the price of an expense account

- Decreasing the price of a liability account

- Decreasing the value of an fairness account

- Decreasing the cost of sales

- Debits are usually recorded at the left

Recording a credit means:

● Decreasing the cost of an asset account

● Decreasing the fee of an rate account

● Increasing the value of a liability account

● Increasing the fee of an fairness account

● Increasing the value of sales

● Credit are usually recorded on the right

The Accrual Method of Bookkeeping

Now which you have a simple expertise of debits and credits and how they're used to document transactions, we are able to talk the accrual method of bookkeeping. When a bookkeeper uses accrual-based totally accounting, he or she will be able to report all transactions primarily based on whilst the transaction happens, as opposed to while cash adjustments hands. For instance, if you make a sale in January, however you don't expect the invoice to be paid until March, a bookkeeper the usage of the accrual method will report the sale in January in place of ready till the bill is paid. Similarly, in case you sell items or services to a client on credit, the accrual approach of bookkeeping allows you to claim the entire sale on the time the transaction takes area, as opposed to recording partial sale on every occasion an installment charge is obtained. Accounting for purchases and charges the use of the accrual approach is similar – for purchases made on credit, the complete rate, no longer simply the quantity of money that modifications fingers – is recorded at the time of the transaction.

Differences among the Accrual Method and the Cash Method

The cash-based totally approach of bookkeeping is primarily based on coins float rather than credit and accounts receivable. When a bookkeeper uses the coins-primarily based method, he'll simplest report transactions whilst coins is paid or obtained. Thus, in case you make a sale, supply the products, and ship an invoice on your customer in January, however your customer does no longer send you a take a look at until March, the bookkeeper will document the sale in March, whilst the payment is received, not in January, whilst the sale turned into made. Similarly, in case you incur costs to deliver goods or services to a customer, a bookkeeper the use of a coins-primarily based method will record the charges on the time you pay for them, in place of making them part of the whole fee of the sale inside the bill to the patron. For instance, when you have to travel to every other metropolis to get admission to personal documents as a part of generating a expert file, the accrual-primarily based method might permit the bookkeeper to defer recording the price of these costs until the invoice is generated; the use of the cash-primarily based method, the every day expenses of any contract might be recorded as they may be incurred and paid by means of the worker.

The vital difference between these methods is that the accrual-primarily based technique can allow your bookkeeper to create a extra accurate photo of your ordinary profits and charges; as a result, it's far a higher approach for enterprise proprietors concerned about tracking their profitability. On the alternative hand, the electricity of the cash-primarily based method of bookkeeping is that you'll have a higher photograph of your day by day cash glide.

You will should perceive which kind of bookkeeping technique you operate while you record your taxes, and if you trade the technique, you'll should notify the Internal Revenue Service via filing a Form 3115, Change in Accounting Method. In addition, if you use an accrual-primarily based technique of accounting, you need to use the double-entry method of bookkeeping. We tested the double-entry technique, which uses debits and credits, above. The subsequent two sections speak the variations between double-access accounting and single-entry accounting.

Single-Entry Bookkeeping (Advantages and Disadvantages)

Single-access bookkeeping may be as compared to retaining track of transaction for your test sign up. Bookkeeping methods that use the unmarried-access method most effective require the bookkeeper to file transactions as they are made, usually payments that are paid from or deposits which can be located into the business enterprise's major bank account. This pretty easy form of bookkeeping is appropriate for small corporations that don't engage in many transactions. The following is an example of a transaction report the usage of the single-access method:

Cash Account

Date	Transaction	Debit	Credit	Balance
January 1, 2020	Balance ahead			$a hundred,000.00
January 5, 2020	Payment acquired	$2,500.00		$102,500.00
January 7, 2020	Rent paid		$750.00	$101,750.00
January 10, 2020	Payroll processed		$40,000.00	$61,750.00

January 12, 2020 Cash   sale
        $eight,000.00 $sixty
nine,750.00

January 15, 2020 Payment   acquired
        $five,500.00
        $75,250.00

January 17, 2020 Equipment   bought
                $2,000.00 $73,250.00

January 20, 2020 Cash   sale
        $five,000.00
        $78,250.00

January 25, 2020 Utilities paid
        $450.00 $seventy
seven,800.00

January 30, 2020 Payment   obtained
        $2,000.00 $79,800.00

Clearly, the gain with unmarried-access bookkeeping is the simplicity of the system. A brief learning curve and the instantaneous accessibility and transferability of this sort of bookkeeping from your studies in private finance to commercial enterprise bookkeeping makes it an appealing choice.

However, if your enterprise has any degree of complexity, or if you require a extra accurate method of tracking your fees, unmarried-access bookkeeping might not address your wishes.

Double-Entry Method (Advantages and Disadvantages)

We mentioned the double-access method inside the phase above entitled, "Recording Debit and Credit in an Account." This type of accounting is glaringly greater complicated that single-access bookkeeping, However, as we have discussed, handiest the double-access approach will can help you file complicated transactions that contain multiple type of account. In addition, double-access accounting can allow you to create a extra correct image of your business enterprise's average monetary condition, which include present day profitability and fee efficiency. These fashions may be used to generate reviews and make predictions for destiny growth, secure investment, and become aware of possibilities for tax breaks or optimization.

Differences Between Excel and Other Software

The machine of debits and credit this is used all through all accounting systems in the modern-day global surroundings turned into developed with the aid of a Franciscan monk lengthy before even the electrical calculator became invented, not to mention the mainframe pc, the digital smartphone, or virtual bookkeeping spreadsheets, apps, and services.

Traditionally, even the most complex accounting and bookkeeping systems had been all maintained by way of getting into transactions with the aid of hand into paper ledgers. Some argue that the area required to preserve paper ledgers and account journals translates into extra economic consciousness and better enterprise development and coverage making selections. There is tons reality to these sentiments; however, it isn't always affordable to expect anybody to return to maintaining paper-based totally records of the company's transactions. Regardless, it is critical to remember the cause and the nature of bookkeeping when you are choosing the equipment and techniques to use to hold track of your agency's price range.

Microsoft Excel spreadsheets are very flexible and can be adapted to a huge kind of makes use of. The phase on Single-Entry Bookkeeping become created the use of an Excel spreadsheet. Considering that bookkeeping and accounting had existed commonly as a paper-based totally practice for maximum of time, it's miles viable to evolve Excel spreadsheets for any form of bookkeeping machine – unmarried-access; double-access; coins-based totally; or accrual-primarily based.

However, a greater suitable use of Excel spreadsheets is to assist the bookkeeper in retaining correct paper-primarily based documents. In such cases, maximum bookkeepers in those instances would in all likelihood be using a single-entry coins-based totally machine.

Bookkeeping software program has reached a excessive stage of improvement, so that a few of the functions discussed in this bankruptcy – balancing double-access transactions and creating reports in accrual-based structures, for instance – have been computerized. However, certainly because the capabilities themselves were automated does now not imply that the software will do the accounting for you. If you input the debits and credit of a transaction in a double-entry system incorrectly, the software may refuse to just accept the access or otherwise warn you to the error, however it's far still the bookkeeper's obligation to ensure the accuracy of all financial statistics entered into the program. Garbage in; garbage out – any accounting or bookkeeping software program you operate is most effective as proper because the accuracy and completeness of the transaction facts you enter into it.

Chapter 2: Handling Assets, Liabilities And Capital

We can not discuss accounting with out using the terms property, liabilities and capital. To grip a full understanding of accounting and bookkeeping, we will cross into information about those terms. You might also have heard terms like this being utilized in discussion and analysis in accounting and bookkeeping.

The phrases property, liabilities and capital are broader in scope than you may have imagined and we are going to have a observe each of those phrases in information.

Assets

In accounting, we consult with belongings as any assets or useful resource owned by the company or employer to be used for destiny transaction and corporations. The sources we term as property are the results of beyond operations, with a view to be used by the business enterprise or commercial enterprise of their transaction of business.

Any homes in bodily or written shape owned by means of the enterprise is referred to as assets and these property may be labeled as present day and noncurrent belongings. The larger a company, the greater belongings it'll have and this asset can be of big gain to the corporation, specially as they may be used to attain coins or obtain loans. The organization seeks to boom its assets because it grows, and tends to collect more land, automobiles, equipment, machinery and different belongings to make bigger a business.

An asset can be top or bad for the enterprise, which relies upon on how the belongings affect the market. In business, you're spending money on acquiring those belongings, in addition to in maintaining those property. So they should be a attention in obtaining assets to determine how they may generate profits for the commercial enterprise either inside the short or long time.

In accounting, the belongings of the employer are recorded inside the double bookkeeping technique. In such a technique, we first ought to determine the type of account the asset falls into and if in that account it is going to be debited or credited.

Current Assets

An asset's sole motive is that it will likely be traded or utilized in change for items or offerings as in coins, and that is referred to as cutting-edge belongings. Cash is an example of modern-day belongings as it can be used for transactions within the next three hundred and sixty five days for salaries, purchase of goods, price for offerings, and so on.

In accounting, belongings are seemed as any belongings or useful resource a good way to be used within the next 12 months or its natural cycle if the employer has one.

To get a whole knowledge of assets, we should observe examples of current assets, which encompass:

1. Cash property, which consist of coins, cash, tests, finances, bills,

financial institution accounts, and so on.

2. Receivables, which include notes, hobby and customer payments, rents, dues earned and claims that deliver income to the company.

three. Another asset is located in inventories, which include gadgets which might be on sale in the organization.

4. All costs paid earlier, which include hire, coverage, resources, etc.

Non-Current Assets

A organization asset is regarded as non-contemporary while it could be used for longer-term purposes and transactions. The long run means that these assets can exceed greater than one year and, in some cases, the life of the employer.

A non-current asset is the opposite of contemporary assets and that they include:

1. Long time period investments, which include shares, bonds and investments in residences are commonplace examples of non-current assets.

2. Landed homes that are used for the commercial enterprise and not up on the market are termed non-modern belongings.

three. Other real estate homes, including places of work, shops, warehouse, a manufacturing facility owned via the enterprise are also regarded as non-current belongings.

four. Office equipment, which incorporates chairs, tables, cabinets, as well as types of equipment, furniture, automobiles and different system fall into this category of non-modern property.

five. Assets that aren't tangible, which encompass goodwill, patent, copyright, emblems and plenty extra.

Liabilities

Liabilities may be appeared as poor capital of a corporation, that are duties that a organisation will ought to pay sometime within the future. When you have got liabilties, those are an indication of claims from outsiders over your organization's belongings and one of those claims is money borrowed to begin or invest within the enterprise.

An asset can come to be a legal responsibility in a organization while it is used for a loan or whilst it drains money out of the business. Liabilities are one critical component of accounting and it is intently watched by way of the buyers to check out the fitness of the enterprise. While assets of a employer are very crucial, what takes away cash from the enterprise is also essential for an investor. A investor will want to recognize the liabilities of the business enterprise and the way it influences the assets of the employer.

A organization would possibly collect many property and might appearance as though it is doing nicely to the untrained eye. But reading the belongings of the organisation and its legal responsibility will let you know extra approximately the agency. This is why investors will by no means approve of the single access account in analyzing a business. The double entry account will comprise all the needed factors that decide the health of the business.

In layman terms, the better the legal responsibility of a employer, the riskier an funding could be in that employer. An accountant will have a look at the report of the enterprise and alert the commercial enterprise owners of the danger of liabilities to the enterprise.

A enterprise must examine its account sheet and watch out for routine liabilities, find a manner to get rid of those habitual liabilities. Liabilities can be dangerous to the commercial enterprise, mainly while they may be routine, which drains out any earnings you may make. If you have got an asset that has emerge as a legal responsibility, you may dispose of the legal responsibility by means of promoting it off and make it into coins belongings to the employer. A assets can grow to be a liability whilst it is of little need, however you continue to need to pay lease or renovation costs on these houses. If you could get rid of these liabilities, then take away them as quickly as possible earlier than they begin to cast off a massive bite of your profit.

We additionally have current and non-contemporary liabilities, simply as we did with the property of a agency.

Current Liabilities

Current liabilities are those liabilities that are short term and expire within 365 days after the stability sheet had been settled. So in essence, all debt owed with current liabilities are expected to be paid on a quick term foundation.

When the modern liabilities of a agency are in excess, the agency is at risk, which means it's far unhealthy as it'd show difficult meeting up with the payments needed. You ought to not allow cutting-edge liabilities to exceed the time that is supposed to elapse due to the fact this can upload charges to the next cycle of the enterprise. Analyze your liabilities and try to cast off liabilities as quickly as viable earlier than they develop and start eating deep into your assets.

Below are some examples of modern-day liabilities so as to expire whilst the enterprise runs its full cycle.

1. Trade transactions and payables, which incorporates interest payable,

rents, gathered costs, notes, and so forth.

2.   Current provisions, along with liabilities that can be measured and paid.

3. Any quick term money borrowed or credit score centers and different debts that need to be paid in less than 365 days.

four. Long term loans which might be due in much less than twelve months or the business cycle.

5. Taxes which might be to be paid in the near future or in the organization cycle.

Non-current Liabilities

A legal responsibility is named non-present day while the company does now not want to make payment within the subsequent two months after the organization's economic cycle. Any long term legal responsibility or duty that does not fall within the company cycle, could consist of:

1. Long time period obligations.

2. Long term loans, bonds, or mortgages that are not predicted to be remitted within the subsequent one year.

3. Taxes or other related liabilities which have been get rid of past the enterprise cycle.

We can agree that long term liabilities are much less dangerous than brief-time period liability for a few apparent motives, which encompass:

- They aren't due in the shortest time so you can make proper preparations for the liabilities.

- They do now not add up to periodical increments if they may be not paid on time like the modern liabilities.

- Non-present day liabilities do now not pile up just like the current liabilities and can be paid in installments with enough time to settle the debt earlier than the due date.

Capital

Capital is the very last property owned via the commercial enterprise minus the liabilities.

A organization can not function without capital. It is needed to make investments and operate the employer. In every circle of enterprise, capital wishes to be reinvested for the growth of the organization. Capital is critical for the growth of the business and it involves received residences.

Capital may be money invested in the commercial enterprise, properties consisting of land, automobiles, equipment, or economic property like bonds, shares and so on. The capital base of a employer is every other vital component buyers need to look. They want to realize how the capital of the organization has advanced over time and the way they were used.

Capital can be reinvested because the business enterprise starts to increase and develop, from the profits made or via searching for different investors. Capital is the bottom of a commercial enterprise for the quantities of capital you spend money on determining your profits on your enterprise. Invest big capital and you will be waiting for high returns, however while you make investments little capital, you would need to exercising some staying power in your commercial enterprise to grow. The opposite is likewise the case with the danger as is regular with any commercial enterprise. When you invest large, you also are taking the threat of losing massive.

In seeking capital to enlarge and develop, you might determine to borrow, for you to be recorded or you can seek traders. And in either case, they'll want you to investigate your books and this is why it's miles crucial to preserve records of the commercial enterprise.

The capital of a enterprise may be suffering from the following:

1. All the contributions made by using the owners of the corporation each at the beginning and all through the walking of the organization.

2. The capital is likewise stricken by the withdrawal, that is made by using the proprietors of the enterprise, together with dividends settlement.

three.   Income that comes into the company.

4.   Expenses incurred by using the agency inside the strolling of the commercial enterprise.

You can see that all of the above points referred to affect the capital of a organisation. While contributions and profits growth the capital of the corporation, costs and other withdrawals lessen the capital of the business.

When the capital of a employer begins to dwindle, then there's cause for alarm as you'll must look for assets to fund operations. This is why we need to be careful of the list above that affect the capital of the business. At this degree, you might need to couple up with traders to put money into your organisation and that is whilst your books and economic report come to be essential.

Keeping tune of the capital glide is some other purpose for having bookkeeping and keeping appropriate data. With these facts, you may continually take a look at how a lot might be had to maintain the operation going and additionally know if the business has enough capital to fulfill up with the call for.

In accounting, the phrases used in describing capital relies upon on the wide variety of people that very own the commercial enterprise. In the case in which the enterprise and the person chargeable for investing in the business is simply one individual, the capital is called proprietor's equity or capital. On the other hand, a enterprise owned via a collection of people is referred to as companion equity or capital, those owned through stockbrokers are referred to as stockbroker equity.

They all bear the risk of the commercial enterprise as long as their capital is in the enterprise and could be fed on first while the company needs similarly capital. If they're now not able to provide you with the capital, they will should search for buyers.

Balance Sheets

The above elements of accounting mentioned on this bankruptcy are used to create the organisation's stability sheet. These accounting sheets have all the equity and liabilities of the corporation stated in sections in step with categories, for easy expertise.

A Balance Sheet is not unusual for massive business and it is straightforward to read and examine for it's miles direct to input data. For a huge corporation, the usage of a stability sheet will cowl all the items that want to be accounted for in a recording.

At a glance of this sort of stability sheet, an accountant can analyze the energy of a enterprise and the cash flow. These documents can be used to determine how sustainable the business is and how you may manage the transaction correctly.

A informed accountant is wanted for a massive business enterprise because they can help in recording and reading account sheets. You can not simply get anyone, just like the owner of the commercial enterprise, to supply an account sheet with all of the operations in mind for huge enterprise. The person handling the account has to have the expert expertise required to stability the sheet.

A suitable stability sheet will calculate the property and capital in one area, even as the liabilities are calculated one after the other, but in a manner that you'll be able to evaluate those factors to be able to research the enterprise.

Balance sheets are one of the gear accountants make use of in reading commercial enterprise necessities well for each the enterprise and investors. It is a complex accounting element that wishes the technical offerings of an expert to interpret and paintings.

The following display the significance of stability sheets:

1. With the stability sheet, you may determine the liquidity of the enterprise, which may be decided from the modern liabilities and modern property as said in a balance sheet account. It is good for a employer while its modern assets are greater than its

present day liabilities in order that the enterprise can attain its short term duties.

The cutting-edge ratio is one of the metrics to calculate the liquidity of a corporation and it is able to be calculated by using

The quick ratio is any other economic metric used inside the calculation of the liquidity of a business enterprise. It measures the capacity of the enterprise to pay its quick time period liabilities and the system for measuring quick ratio is

Quick Ratio=

2. With a accurate balance sheet, you may calculate the leverage of a enterprise and this leverage can be used to determine the monetary

danger the agency can take. The stability sheet gives the accountant all he calls for to exercise session the leverage of the agency and how it is able to be of use to the enterprise.

three. The efficiency of the enterprise can easily be determined the use of the profits of the organisation. Calculating the asset turnover ratio gives us an idea of ways the corporation converts assets into revenue. This suggests us how accurate the organisation is in turning its investment around to carry earnings into the business.

The fixed asset ratio is a financial metric used to calculate how fast the commercial enterprise can generate income with its property.

4. With the stability sheet, you may calculate the charge of returns of

property and fairness, that is critical to reveal the boom of the commercial enterprise.

Return of equity, that's measured in probabilities, is the internet income divided by means of the shareholder's equity. This metric is crucial in measuring the ability of the enterprise to convert belongings to income, that's more likely the shareholder's funding and the way they can generate profit for the enterprise. The return of equity makes use of the stability sheet and the declaration of account.

You can use those to analyze your assets, liabilities and capital in managing the accounting of the enterprise. With an accountant, the commercial enterprise can be sustained with analytical information acquired from the statistics acquired as proven above.

This type of information can not be obtained with single entry bookkeeping however as a substitute with double access bookkeeping where you could enter all of the facts used in dealing with the belongings, liabilities and capital of the business.

Chapter 3: Using Ledgers And Journals To Track Business Activity

Before we can begin to apprehend the financial reviews, we need to look at wherein the data comes from. We can begin with the magazine entries which might be made via the business and when the ones entries are published to the ledgers. Next, we will then have a look at how we are able to song the ones transactions. Knowing in which the transactions got here from and wherein they are listed within the financial reviews will assist you better apprehend the reviews which might be created.

Financial Journals

Most of the time while we talk approximately journaling in accounting and bookkeeping we discuss with the General Journal.

How frequently have you ever looked at the General Journal and gotten misplaced on how the commercial enterprise is sincerely doing? Don't fear! If you stated loads or all of the time then you aren't alone. That is why in bookkeeping, together with the General Journal, you have six additional journals. They are:

Cash Receipts Journal (CRJ)

Cash Payments Journal (CPJ)

Sales Journal (SJ)

Sales Returns Journal (SRJ)

Purchase Journal (PJ)

Purchase Returns Journal (PRJ)

General Journal (GJ)

Let's study each of the seven journals to get a higher knowledge. In the examples, you'll additionally see the ref discipline. There can be references there that don't correspond to a magazine. That is because they may correspond to a specific ledger. We could be talking about ledgers later in this chapter.

Remember, if you are the use of accounting software then all that is done for you via that software program. However, it's far pleasant to realize the basics so that you can higher recognize where the economic reviews are coming from.

Cash Receipts Journal (CRJ)

When you obtain coins, you will record it within the Cash Receipts Journal. The categories of the CRJ are:

Date

Details

Ref.

Bank

Income

Debtors

Sundry

When you look at the CRJ, you'll see 3 major classes: The financial institution is the entire of every line and shows how a lot coins become received. Income is taken from receipts where you delivered in money, while debtors is when you have a receipt wherein you paid out money. The class "sundry" is a word which means "various," miscellaneous," or "popular."

Here is an example of a CRJ:

DATE	DETAILS	REF	BANK	INCOME	DEBTORS	SUNDRY
1	Capital	S1	15,000	-	-	15,000
7	Loan	S2	five,000	-	-	5,000
12	Service rendered	L1	10,500	10,500	-	-
30	Smiths	L2	five,000	-	5,000	-
Total			35,500	10,500	five,000	20,000

Cash Payments Journal (CPJ)

Much like the CRJ, the Cash Payments Journal shows in which the coins has been paid out of the commercial enterprise. The classes of the CPJ are:

Date

Details

Ref.

Expenses

Creditors

Sundry

Bank

If you note, the kinds are the identical except for income is now costs, the Debtors is now Creditors, and the bank category is now on the cease. Here is an example of a CPJ:

DATE	DETAILS	REF	EXPENSES	CREDITORS	SUNDRY	BANK
8	Equipment purchased	A1	-	-	12,000	12,000
9	Drawings	S3	-	-	500	500
12	Salary	E1	4,000	-	-	4,000
13	Telephone enterprise	L2	-	2 hundred	-	two hundred
15	Loan repayment	S4	-	-	4,000	four,000
Totals			four,000	200	16,500	20,seven-hundred

Keep in mind that in case you pick the use of a cash e-book, it's far a combination of the SRJ and the SPJ. This

67

will allow for the coins e-book to reveal all receipts and bills collectively.

If your business has a petty cash fund, you may keep song of this fund with extra journals and use the identical layout as the CRJ and the CPJ.

Sales Journal (SJ)

Whether you're are imparting offerings, merchandise, or each, I assume we will agree that income are essential. That's why a Sales Journal is a extremely good device to have. Remember that most effective the profits on credit score might be recorded inside the SJ. Once it's far paid and your commercial enterprise receives cash for the provider, then it is going to be recorded within the cash receipts magazine.

The classes for the SJ:

Date

Debtor

Ref.

Services rendered

Here is an instance of what a Sales Journal may also look like:

DATE	DEBTOR	REF	SERVICE RENDERED
8	Smiths	L2	5,000
Total			5,000

Sales Returns Journal (SRL)

If you have got a business enterprise that has products, you on occasion address lower back products. You will use the Sales Returns Journal to music the returns that have been at the beginning bought.

The categories within the SRL are:

Date

Debtor

Ref.

Sales returns

Here is an instance of what an SRL may additionally seem like:

DATE	DEBTOR	REF	SALES RETURNS
sixteen	J. Jacobs	R1	300
Total			three hundred

Purchases Journal (PJ)

When your business has inventory, you may actually have a Purchases Journal. This journal is used while your business purchases inventory on credit. Remember, a PJ simplest applies to stock. Therefore, now not all belongings are recorded here. Only stock purchased on credit could be recorded within the PJ.

The categories on a Purchases Journal are:

Date

Creditor

Ref.

Purchases

Here is what a Purchases Journal may appear like:

DATE	CREDITOR	REF	PURCHASES
three	J.P. Manufacturers	P1	5,500
five	Wood Importers Inc.	P2	1,500
Total			7,000

Purchases Returns Journal (PRJ)

Just like the SRJ, the Purchases Returns Journal is for recording merchandise that your enterprise purchased on credit score and then needed to return to the products.

The categories for the PRJ are:

Date

Creditor

Ref.

Purchases returns

Here is an example of what a Purchases Returns Journal can also appear to be:

DATE CREDITOR   REF   PURCHASES RETURNS

3   J.P. Manufacturers   P1   a hundred

five   Wood Importers Inc.   P2
      1,500

Total   1,600

General Journal (GJ)

So typically, we talk about the General Journal because it holds all of the transaction a business makes. When you think about it, by means of the use of that definition of a standard magazine you're referring to all seven journals. However, the General Ledger does that very factor. That is proper! The General Journal has all of the transactions that don't match into the opposite six journals.

The layout is easy. It includes:

Date

Description

Ref.

Debit

Credit

Here is an example of what a primary magazine can also look like:

DATE	DISCRIPTION	REF	DEBIT	CREDIT
Apr 2	Description for the Debit		1,000	
	Indent the description for the Credit(s)			1,000
sixteen	Description for the Debit		7,000	
	Indent the outline for the Credit(s)			7,000
19	Description for the Debit		3,000	

Indent the description for the Credit(s)   three,000

Totals   11,000

eleven,000

When running with the general magazine, always do not forget the Debits and Credits need to equal.

The Ledgers

For bookkeeping and double-access accounting there are 3 essential categories of ledgers we need to study.

General Ledger (GL)

Accounts Receivable Ledger (ARL)

Accounts Payable Ledger (APL)

You might imagine that it's far a waste of time to record the entries two times. You will find that just because you have got journaled the transactions in one of the seven journals it's miles useful to organize the transactions into the ledger money owed as well.

General Ledger (GL)

When you installation your enterprise bookkeeping, a Chart of Accounts become created. Each account in this Chart of Accounts has a Ref range assigned to it. This reference is available in available for each the Journals and the Ledgers. For each account at the Chart of Accounts you'll have a General Ledger for the account. In each General Ledger, you'll have both a Debit or Credit everyday stability.

In the seven journals, you'll file the ledger or associated magazine within the ref subject. In the ledgers, you may file the corresponding journal in the ref field.

Let's examine the General Journal in your commercial enterprise's Cash account.

Account: Cash - Ref: a hundred

DATE	DESCRIPTION	REF	DEBIT	CREDIT
Apr 1	Opening Balance		4,500	
1		J1	25.00	
four		J1		one hundred eighty.00
four		J1	250.00	
eight		J2		a hundred forty five.00
10		J2	25.00	

Total Note: End of Month totals)
    4,285

The total is calculated on the cease of each month and carried ahead to the following month as the brand new opening stability. There might be a ledger for every account at the Chart of Accounts.

Accounts Receivable Ledger (ARL) and Accounts Payable Ledger (APL)

The Accounts Receivable and Accounts Payable Ledgers are subsidiary ledger debts. These are debts that are further to the General Ledgers however are particularly for monitoring the receivables and payables.

You may have more than one bills of vendors who owe you money otherwise you owe money too. Each account can have their personal ledger.

Accounts Receivable will have a Debit normal balance even as Accounts Payable can have a Credit everyday stability.

Here is an example of each form of ledger:

Debtor: A. Franklin - Ref: AR-F

DATE	REF	DEBIT	CREDIT	BALANCE
July 18	Terms 60 days	SJ1	one hundred fifty.00	one hundred fifty.00
27	Terms 30 days	SJ1	a hundred ninety.00	340.00

Creditor: Smiths ManufacturerRef: AP-S

DATE	REF	DEBIT	CREDIT	BALANCE
July 14 Terms 60 days	SJ1	60.00		60.00
21 Terms 30 days	SJ1	100.00		a hundred and sixty.00

Tracking Transactions

Now that we've got the journals and the ledgers, how can we song all the pastime this is going on? It is easy. Look at the Ref column. The Ref column will display the link among the seven journals and the ledgers from the Chart of Accounts.

In addition to the journals and ledgers, you will notice that the profits announcement (profit and loss announcement) and the balance sheet will be made out of the General Ledgers.

Chapter 4: Why Bookkeeping Is Important For Business

1. Improved economic analysis and control

Cash float management is something that your commercial enterprise have to start focussing on proper away. Once your invoices are delayed, there will be 0 comply with-americaon purchaser payments. Falling out on the supplier's listing of customers will eventually crash you down. However, all this may be corrected with bookkeeping. With accurate bookkeeping, you may systematize your comply with-usaand invoicing, even as making on-time payments to suppliers.

2. Fulfil your tax responsibilities on time

Bookkeeping will let you preserve a music on all the data and documents required to accomplish your annual taxes. When the time for tax comes, you will now not need to rush anywhere to hunt to your bills or attempt to keep in mind your expenses. An organized Balance Sheet, Profit & Loss and Cash Flow also makes submitting your Tax Returns plenty simpler. Your tax guide can also sooner or later give you some sound tax recommendation as an alternative correcting incorrect entries to your financial statements.

3. Enjoy clean reporting on your traders

With everyday and accurate bookkeeping, you will now not want to fear approximately reporting to your investors and sharing the economic fame of your enterprise. From graphs to charts and the lists of facts, you may easily present everything to your investor proper out of your accounting books.

four. Make knowledgeable enterprise plans

With the Balance Sheet and Profit & Loss statements, you can take a look at in case your company is at the right track financially. Based on your financial status, you can make knowledgeable and effective enterprise plans.

5. Keep a proper file, as required by means of the Law

With bookkeeping, you can keep a record of all of your financial dealings and maintain the whole thing prepared proper out of your massive to small invoices. This makes the retrieving procedure extraordinarily easy, once the time for auditing comes.

To obtain all of the above, you may outsource bookkeeping and accounting to a professional organization. This way, you can always hold the economic components of your enterprise intact and organized. Bookkeeping can show you the distinction among bankruptcy and fulfillment. It can also literally suggest financial savings in hundreds of greenbacks on your business enterprise.

Chapter 5: How To Adjust Any Entry

As you're working with your small business, you may discover that there are instances when you need to modify some of the entries which you installed for bookkeeping. These magazine entries can be able to show your accounting information into accrual-based accounting. These are the entries that you may need to make prior to issuing the financial statements.

In many instances, when you need to adjust an entry, you're doing it because you want to restoration a number of your charges. However, you could want to use this for other matters as nicely, such as making adjustments for sales. Basically, there are two eventualities in which adjusting access is needed before the economic statements are issued, and those encompass the following:

When not anything has been placed into the accounting facts for a certain sales or prices. These revenues or costs did occur, and they ought to be covered inside the modern stability sheet or income statement for that length, so an adjustment is necessary.

When there has been an entry into the facts, but the quantity needs to be divided up as it occurs through more than one accounting period.

 Asset Accounts

Any time that you are trying to make a few adjustments to the entries which you have, you want to take the time to guarantee that both the profits assertion and the stability sheet are accomplished properly in order that they test out with every other. While we can talk approximately both of these monetary statements in a later bankruptcy, this basically manner that each those statements want to be up to date based totally at the accrual foundation of accounting.

The quality way to undergo and do this is to take a look at and then review each of the balances which can be on your balance sheet. Let's take a look at the following example after which ruin it down to get a better idea of what is going on. Remember, that is primarily based at the account balances that had been completed before any of the adjustments have been added. The unique areas that we are able to focus on right here will encompass the following:

Cash: $1,800

Accounts Receivable: $4,six hundred

Allowance for doubtful money owed: $0

Supplies: $1,100

Prepared coverage: $1,500

Accumulated depreciation system: $7,500

Equipment: $25,000

Let's smash this down now that we've all of the numbers. Looking at the general ledger, we'll see that the cash account is displaying there is a balance of $1,800 in cash. However, before you use this facts to create your stability sheet, there are two questions which you want to invite yourself. First, ask whether or not the $1,800 is the real sum of money or no longer? Second, ask if this concurs with what became figured primarily based to your bank reconciliation.

If the coins doesn't fit with what you discovered out while you did the bank reconciliation, then you definately want to go through and make a few modifications in order that the stability sheet has the proper data. Some examples of wanting to do this would be to check printing costs, banking costs, or service fees. These entries need to be added to the coins account in order that it suits up with your financial institution statements.

Then you need to check the money owed receivable. For this account, you want to test any of the unpaid invoices that you have. These can be discovered at the subsidiary ledger for bills receivable. For this, we're going to assume that the $4,six hundred that we had above is correct for all the quantities that have been not paid as of yet.

The stability sheets will want to report all the quantities. This need to additionally consist of the cash that has not yet been paid but is still due to the business. This can also go for all of the revenue that has been billed at that point as properly. After a evaluation, you discover that $three,000 of services has been earned. This became dated as something that came about on December 31, however it changed into not billed till January 20. In order to have that statistics show up for your December economic statements, you'll want to undergo and make an adjusting access.

Remember that while you do your entries, they all need to have at the least one credit and one debit. The two bills that you might do in this may be the carrier sales and the money owed receivable. The bills receivable can have the ordinary debit balance, and it will be a part of your balance sheet bills. The service sales have a normal credit stability and also part of the earnings assertion bills.

When we test the previous stability that we had of $4,six hundred for this region after which we make the adjusting access for the $3,000 that needs to be added in, then the brand new balance on this account is going to be $7,600.

Now we need to work at the allowances for dubious bills. If you check your records right here, you'll note that this account isn't always one this is listed for your stability sheet. The reason for this is because it has a stability of $0. It is not unusual for an account that has a stability of $zero to not show up on the balance sheet because it's miles just going to pretty a good deal soak up area.

At one point, there is a possibility that your business has a few accounts that have now not been accrued. The reasons for this may vary. Instead of decreasing the accounts receivable by means of issuing a credit on the ledgers, you will add it to this category.

To take a look at this, let's say that your enterprise has $six hundred that isn't always going to be accrued. This way which you would need to document that $six hundred within the allowance for doubtful account. There are going to be debts that want to be delivered in for this transaction. You will have this allowance for dubious accounts at the balance sheet, and this account can have a credit ordinary stability. Then the other account goes to be the terrible debts price that is on the earnings declaration. This account goes to have a ordinary debit stability.

As you go through your stability sheet, you need to keep in mind which accounts are going to be affected and which of them can have either a regular debit or credit score. From right here, you have to make an effort and practice doing all your very own bookkeeping. Try to parent out the relaxation of the adjusting entries for the asset accounts. These are the numbers that you must use for purchasing this finished and getting some exercise:

Supplies are $1,one hundred.

Adjusting access is $275. The stability for materials may be $725 and the debts that you will use to get this performed may be resources and substances rate.

Prepaid coverage is $1,500.

The adjusting access is going to be $900. The balance for this pay as you go insurance may be $600, and the money owed that you may use are coverage rate and pay as you go coverage.

Equipment is $25,000.

You do no longer want to do any adjusting entries right here.

Accumulated depreciation gadget is $7,500.

Adjusting access goes to be $15,000. The balance for the amassed depreciation gadget goes to be $nine,000, and the bills that you may use for this one may be the accrued depreciation device and the depreciation cost device.

Adjusting the Entries with Liability Accounts

As you take a evaluation of the accounts which can be in your stability sheet, it isn't enough to simply test the property and then prevent there. The liability accounts have to also be reviewed. You need to undergo and test out these money owed using the equal methods that you used with the property. The steps to doing this will include the subsequent:

Notes payable: $5,000

There is no adjusting access that is wanted right here.

Interest payable: $0

Adjusting access is $25. The stability for the interest payable is going to be $25, and the debts which might be concerned with this are the hobby rate and the interest payable.

Accounts payable: $2,500

Adjusting entry is $1,000. The stability for the debts payable may be $3,500 and the bills involved are accounts payable and repairs and protection expense.

Wages payable is $1,two hundred.

Adjusting entry is $300. The balance of wages payable is going to be $1,500, and the money owed that you will use with this one are the wages payable and the wages price.

Unearned revenues will be $1,three hundred.

Adjusting access is $800. The balance on your unearned sales will be $500, and the money owed involved will encompass unearned sales and provider sales.

When you do this, don't forget that the ordinary balance for each of the account goes to be affected. As you undergo and alter the entries, and when you do not recognise the regular stability for both transactions, you have to try and find the only that you do understand. There goes to be a credit score and debit for each transaction made continually. If it has a credit normal balance after which the adjustment finally ends up growing the account, you then want to additionally go through and debit the alternative account.

Special gadgets: There are some events that can every now and then be charged in opposition to the earnings of the corporation. The organization can pick out those as discontinued operations, unusual gadgets, or restructuring prices. These are write-offs that must simply be one-time activities. Any investor that looks at your organization have to examine these gadgets and recall them whilst searching at a company because now and again, they could distort the assessment.

Net earnings: This is also known as the net profits or the internet income. This goes to be the bottom line for the business enterprise, and it is going to be the most not unusual indicator of ways worthwhile the business enterprise is. If the fees exceed the profits, then you'll have a net loss. After that, the enterprise will pay out the dividends that are preferred stockholders if there are any, after which the net profits goes to add to the fairness position of the organization and turns into retained income. There is occasionally a few supplemental facts supplied for net earnings on the premise of ability conversion of shares, basis of stocks tremendous, and warrants.

Comprehensive income: This concept is going to do not forget the consequences of a few matters including unrealized profits and losses, the minimum pension legal responsibility, foreign currency modifications, and more. The funding network is broadly speaking going to keep focusing on the net income discern that we pointed out before. The adjustment items that include comprehensive earnings will all relate to a marketplace that is volatile or an monetary event this is out of manage of the control at the time. The impact at that precise time can be massive, but over the years, they may be going to even out and received't count that plenty.

Chapter 6: Then one tax management Strategy To Save Money

Companies have the hazard to lessen the amount of taxes that they have to pay closer to the IRS. In this bankruptcy, we are able to have a look at the different things that you can do to reduce how an awful lot tax you pay.

Choose the right form of enterprise

First off, begin by means of picking the right term to suit your commercial enterprise into. That is, make certain whether you need to be a sole owner or an LLC. You need to pick the right one for you to pay the right tax. Don't be below the impact that you can choose something you suspect sounds accurate. You must choose something that will help you avail tax advantages.

For instance, a sole proprietor can take gain of many deductions at the same time as submitting for taxes whereas individuals of an LLC will not be held for my part vulnerable to any money owed that the enterprise owes.

Work possibility tax credit score

Work opportunity tax credit refers to a tax deduction that you can avail for hiring a battle veteran or someone that has confronted huge problems in finding a job to in shape their cadre. You can show the IRS their employment letter and also the revenue that you pay them. The amount paid will be deducted from your tax. There is a restriction to what number of you could appoint or use as a way to reduce your agency's tax.

Retirement benefits

You can provide retirement advantages to your employees for you to help you store on taxes. You ought to pick the fine plans that healthy your commercial enterprise. Retirement benefits can range from imparting a monthly pension to paying month-to-month payments that your personnel would possibly incur once they retire. So, you have to choose the excellent plans and assist keep on a large quantity of taxes which you might ought to pay to the IRS.

Unify

If you have a slew of organizations, then you could recollect bringing all of them underneath a single roof, as that will help you pay a unique tax. You don't have to fear approximately submitting one-of-a-kind papers for every individual organization. You can record for simply one and be achieved with it very quickly in any respect. You can in fact, offset the losses of a company with the profits of any other. You can also increase the wide variety of deductions which you make. Doing so will substantially help you stay with a big profit at the quit and might not should pay up as many taxes.

Independent contractors

There is an advantage to employing unbiased contractors in place of personnel. If you're going for walks a enterprise or organization, then you may recall employing impartial contractors, as they'll assist you avoid paying payroll taxes. This is terrific for all the ones small enterprise which are trying to capitalize on small profits. You can also hire freelancers if you want.

Hiring circle of relatives

It is a superb concept so as to hire your children and own family individuals to work for you. Doing so will assist you avoid paying them an allowance and you can deduct their salaries out of your tax returns. It need not always be your kith and family and may be cousins, aunts, uncles etc. This is particularly beneficial for sole proprietors. They will no longer owe any social protection or Medicare taxes on their children's salaries, in order to show to be quite fantastic.

Write off assets two times

Better known as a present hire lower back, you can write off an asset like a vehicle twice. Like a automobile that you use to your commercial enterprise, that's absolutely depreciated. Its market value stands at $15,000. You determine to rent it out for your spouse for $500 a month. You can then avail a benefit of

$6,000, which can be deducted out of your taxation. Travel/ clinical charges

You can take benefit of tour and scientific fees reimbursements. And it isn't always simply yours that you could reimburse, you could reimburse your enterprise accomplice's, spouses, children's, established's and so on. You can produce suitable receipts and avail the deductions.

Renting your home

If you very own a residence, then you may rent it out to an S corporation and earn tax-unfastened earnings from it. You can lease it out to a agency for approximately 14 days a month to conduct meetings and seminars etc. And now not declare it. But remember there's a restriction to how many human beings can occupy it at any given point in time. Also, you need to specify to the company that there may be no entertainment supplied for the duration of the conferences. If you own an S enterprise then you may use your house for conferences and deduct hire to your self from corporation debts.

Telephone/ Internet payments

It is a common exercise amongst sole proprietors to use their smartphone for professional and private makes use of after which deduct the smartphone invoice from their business taxes. You can also maintain two distinctive phones if you want and use the payments to avail a relief. The identical extends to any stationery and different matters which you buy in your business enterprise on a ordinary foundation.

Tax Planning

All marketers which are planning to form their startups and small business proprietors must apprehend the fundamentals of taxation to behave for that reason, with the tax legal guidelines applied by federal and nation authority.

Small companies can try to achieve the help of tax professionals and experts to make sure a a success tax return. Moreover, they also can undertake numerous tax making plans strategies and methods at some point of the monetary year

for higher returns. If anyone can't manage to pay for one, then the Internal Revenue Services and State Revenue branch contains a wide form of assets available to them to help the small business enterprise proprietors with tax making plans.

Tax making plans may be defined as the sports that a corporation may adopt to maximise its tax liabilities to growth the possibilities and to ensure to benefit all viable allowances, deductions, exemptions, and exclusions available. In brief, it's far the process of operating together inside the maximum tax-green way to lessen the full tax invoice a firm is liable to pay in a fiscal year.

Furthermore, it may additionally be referred to as a element of an analysis of the financial repute a commercial enterprise may have in their cutting-edge state of affairs or with the approaching plans drafted together with the forecasted goal of growing return on capital hired.

Calling tax planning as an critical part of a monetary plan would now not be incorrect. Because by some means a enterprise manages to break out from one tax bracket to every other, this results in a discount in tax amount or a fall within the tax rate it's far vulnerable to pay. As nicely as it contributes to the maximization of the potential of an entrepreneur to draft an awesome retirement plan, and also are essential for the achievement of the commercial enterprise.

How Tax Planning Works

Tax planning covers up many problems faced through maximum of the corporations. Especially whilst planning and forecasting destiny financial positions of their entity. The technique includes several issues inclusive of the timing of income, length, when the purchase could be made, and planning for different expenses in opposition to the modern-day yr earned sales. It is also determined within the procedure that for destiny expansion which sources of finance and funding would be decided on and ambitions for the maximum suitable retirement plan.

All the crucial selections made in this making plans system without delay or indirectly affect the tax submitting popularity of companies and deductions to create the exceptional feasible final results.

Types of Taxes to be Considered within the Tax Planning

Also, mention before, tax planning techniques are normally employed to assist a business in achieving its economic and non-financial business dreams and goals. There are many blessings that an corporation is probably to advantage through tax making plans, and this is one predominant motive why experts emphasis loads on its importance, specially in the case of small businesses.

In most nations, the tax laws and allowances keep on changing from time-to-time. Hence, it is usually advisable for businesses to often review their strategies. The tax making plans system may not affect your whole tax shape, and rather there are few areas wherein the system of an expert might be able to advantage your commercial enterprise, reducing the quantity of tax liability.

Capital Gains Tax

Planning for the capital benefit tax means taking various of things into consideration, including which asset is being to and who is going to be the next proprietor of the asset. In such occasions, you may require the help of a tax planner to do the calculation for you, and notify you about the property that are exempted and might cause a discount in the amount of tax payable.

Corporate tax

Usually, corporate tax or the tax on earnings is taken into consideration to be one of the better fees a profitable business enterprise has to bear. Therefore, corporate tax planning is important for each small and huge corporations, therefore allowing them to maintain a better margin of income or extracting extra price from the commercial enterprise.

Corporate Tax Planning Includes

Deferring profits or income

Bringing ahead prices

Capital allowances

International Tax

No depend, in case you are running a business globally, or are making plans to begin one inside the u . S ., you are constrained or certain to observe the limitations set by means of the tax legal guidelines. International tax planning might help you to legally avoid such laws and allow you to save neighborhood taxes in addition to the taxes levied on international commercial enterprise.

International Tax Planning Includes

The due date of tax bills to determine when to pay

Using the tax deferral possibilities and tax rebates

Gaining the foreign tax credits and incentives

Avoiding the case of double taxation Dividend/Year-quit Tax Planning

Are you making plans to keep returned a sizeable profit margin for your employer, however don't recognise the way to do that? Then you could require a tax professional or planner who could advocate you on the way to maximize your go back by lowering the amount of tax liability. Many advise that it is able to be wise to attract out a huge amount as dividends given to the proprietors. However, tax experts may be capable of recommend you at the maximum tax-efficient way to reward your self and for your personnel.

Inheritance Tax

Your successors or family contributors can be required to pay inheritance tax when you are dead, which may also reduce the quantity of your property or wealth you have amassed in your life that ends up being handed on to your loved ones or felony heirs. There are many solutions and techniques available to keep away from the inheritance tax consisting of;

Giving your private home and acquired assets as a present to your loved ones

Downsizing

 Remortgaging & insurance options are to be had Tax Planning for Individuals

It is only a delusion that tax planning is the first-class choice best for huge corporations. Rather private people can also keep their accumulated wealth through adopting an intensive tax making plans system.

Individual Tax Planning Includes

Income taxes

Gifting kids

Gifting family contributors

Property

Pensions

Why is Tax Planning for Small Businesses Important?

Many small groups and marketers with lack of enjoy consult from taxation corporations and professionals to undertake a tax-efficient approach that can assist them with the discount within the tax quantity they may be vulnerable to pay. In any condition, those experts will insist you to consciousness extra on tax making plans. It is due to the fact it is the most distinguished and beneficial tool to be used to lessen the amount of your taxable income. The procedure of tax making plans would bring about lowering the tax fee concern on your profits or earned earnings by using moving it from one tax bracket to any other or from the excessive charge to a lower one. Moreover, it'd allow you to utilize any tax credit score or incentive that may be to be had.

Allows You to Make Smart Year-End Decisions

Till now, you've got discovered a lot about taxes, its differing types, exclusive structures, and systems. Being an proprietor of a small enterprise, now is the time to examine extra approximately tax planning. It could be plenty better if, as quickly as feasible, you may comprehend the importance of tax making plans in your monetary operations, growing the profitability and returns of the enterprise.

You can decide the significance of tax making plans by means of the truth that it plays a important part in getting your economic information and data up to date, in particular on the end of a fiscal year, when you have to report taxes on your earned earnings in opposition to costs. It additionally permits you to see wherein your company profits and losses stand, permitting you to make the simplest selection in much less time. A smart choice can bring about the possible minimization of your tax liabilities.

However, many business proprietors these days are less likely to take benefit in their hired sellers and accountants for tax making plans purposes. Anyone who is not paying attention or doesn't bear in mind tax planning as an vital step, as a end result, she or he would possibly leave out the tax-saving opportunity, which wishes to be applied earlier than the financial or monetary yr ends.

Other than the tax-saving benefits that you'll be capable of advantage, thru tax planning, there are other advantages too, like you will get a head start on your taxation. The word of head begin is used, in the sense that to draft an effective tax plan, initially, you'll assessment your books of money owed. Next, you will set all of the records and records on the tune.

Therefore, within the method of tax planning, you is probably capable of do a number of those responsibilities that in different cases could have still been ignored. In the situation, you might additionally create a list of gadgets that you're going to need at the start of the next year, and so now you have got enough time to collect the information, instead of developing a fuss in the final second.

The list of benefits, contributing to the importance of tax planning doesn't simply give up right here, alternatively there are manner too many. So it's miles smart no longer to disregard it.

Common Mistakes Made by Small Business on Tax Planning

The proprietors of small organizations are regularly seen to tackle a lot of burden with the entire agency upon their shoulders. It is because they're no longer in-fee of handiest one however of a couple of departments, whether or not it is advertising, personnel and group of workers control, development of product, or accounting practices. They are continually observed busy running of their enterprise and so they're left with much less time available for them to work at the management in their corporate taxes.

Amongst the maximum ordinary errors that the proprietors of small groups do whilst getting ready a tax plan is to treat it as an exercise that is to be done after the yr-stop. Many of them do their plan for his or her taxation earlier than the give up of the year, and therefore, it creates no real trade and left no capacity opportunity to affect the taxable profits. It is probably true for individuals who pay their taxes on the coins foundation as on this, the timing while the cash receipts are received or what is the due date to pay them and payment to providers can probably create a considerable effect at the contemporary yr's profits. For example, taxpayers who pay on a coins foundation have the possibility to deduct costs which can be pay as you go until they do no longer exceed the length of twelve months or past the end of the subsequent tax yr.

Another mistake completed by means of the proprietors of small businesses is after they have to face failure in spotting other important vital necessities that exists, and are associated with their business enterprise. They are required to sign up their seller for sales tax, must prepare the once a year forms along with the only 1099-MISC for his or her carriers, and ought to

appropriately report, highlighting the distinction between their hired body of workers contributors and subcontractors. If a enterprise fails to prepare their tax filings and plans in line with the necessities that relates to the topics cited above, then as a result, it may divulge its company owner to the unexpected burden of tax liabilities.

The rate of tax problem for your profits or the tax bracket your company earnings lie relies upon at the commercial enterprise structure or the type of enterprise you very own and operate. Likewise, the procedure of tax making plans also depends in your company structure.

In summary, the smarter you propose for taxation, the lesser the amount or the fee of taxes you may be vulnerable to pay, however it's no longer one time, instead it's an ongoing manner this is going to take you sufficient time. If you do no longer apprehend or suppose that you cannot hold the essential part of it, then it is suggested which you ought to consult from a tax professional and specialists or need to conduct a couple of meeting session with your tax advisor and specialists inside a unmarried 12 months.

You have to gift your latest or ultra-modern financial statements and need to have a discussion in your innovative thoughts regards the imminent tasks, purchases, staffing, and different adjustments. It will allow your hired or employed tax guide and experts that after and how they let you in drafting an powerful tax plan that can beautify your retained profit inside the present day financial 12 months and in the future.

Chapter 7: Classification Of Accounts

Types of Accounts

What is an account? An account is any man or woman or collective file of a person, any particular move of income, and any form of fee of a organization or an enterprise. The account serves as a document for any form of monetary transaction and is constantly expressed in monetary terms. Learning approximately the one-of-a-kind types of accounts and dealing with them is one of the most critical aspects of bookkeeping. Although it could sound quite simple, there are one-of-a-kind styles of accounts for extraordinary business transactions. There are three exceptional forms of commercial enterprise transactions.

• All kinds of transactions which might be associated with person human beings.

• All styles of transactions which are related to profits and expenditure.

• All styles of transactions which are associated with the belongings or residences of a firm/organization.

The 3 classes of debts are maintained to report the transactions of a business in correspondence to the one of a kind categories of transactions, as discussed above. These accounts also are called non-public money owed, nominal debts, and real money owed. As we progress thru this bankruptcy, you will research greater about every of those 3 extraordinary styles of debts. You will simplest be able to completely understand the policies of debit and credit on bookkeeping if you realize how these exceptional types of debts paintings.

Personal Account

All the economic transactions and dealing that a enterprise is a part of with different individuals or business corporations fall beneath the class of private accounts. A separate personal account is opened for every such man or woman or company to report all the transactions that take place or might also take area inside the future. Whenever this kind of organization or character gets any precise benefit, their money owed might be debited with that specific benefit, and also, their money owed can be credited every time they communicate any kind of advantage closer to the host company.

There are four distinctive styles of non-public money owed, and they may be as follows:

Natural Personal Account

A herbal private account consists of accounts of different providers, owners, creditors, or any other person person.

Artificial Personal Account

An artificial personal account includes all styles of insurance bills, financial institution money owed, debts of limited businesses, government bills, or even any club's money owed. Every time an account is created for the cause of representing a specific person or a particular institution of individuals, it's also known as a consultant private account. In maximum business books, the names of the actual parties will appear. Since they're generally the equal nature, and the transactions are in large numbers, all the amounts which are standing in opposition to those money owed might be introduced under one precise not unusual header or title. For instance, if a particular company has no longer been capable of make its month-to-month hire bills for a couple of months, then a brand new unmarried account might be created beneath the company's facts below the common head of 1 exceptional rent account. Any rental bills that could additionally be because of other one of a kind landlords might be recorded under this account. Unexpired coverage accounts, pay as you go rent bills, interest pay as you go debts, and exquisite interest debts are some other examples of representative non-public bills.

Real Account

A actual account, also called a belongings account, is used for recording any monetary transactions in or handling assets, possessions, and belongings. These debts often represent exclusive objects which can be more or much less tangible, and which preserve a huge monetary fee. For each unique type of belongings or asset that a company or organisation owns, a separate real account will be maintained for it. Some commonplace matters which might be protected in actual accounts or property accounts are fixtures, gadget, missionary, or other such belongings. Real accounts are maintained so one can report the particulars of every transaction this is given away or obtained by means of the firm so that you will without difficulty keep song of the cost of the assets that the corporation holds at any specific point in time. Whenever the corporation acquires or receives any particular asset or keeping, the financial fee of that asset might be debited into the concerned account, and it is going to be deducted whenever the said asset is given away. You will study extra approximately the policies of debit and credit within the drawing close chapters. Real debts may be further categorized into actual tangible debts and real intangible bills.

A actual tangible account is maintained to record all accounts of belongings which are tangible, may be measured, filed, purchased, and bought. It basically serves to preserve a document of all tangible belongings. Some common examples of actual tangible money owed consist of constructing debts, inventory bills, cash debts, land money owed, and other such tangible property bills.

A real intangible account is used for keeping track of all belongings or possessions/holdings that a commercial enterprise owns, which are intangible in nature. Assets like Goodwill, emblems, patents, and different copyright possessions that don't always have any physical life but have considerable financial cost are covered in real intangible accounts.

Nominal Accounts

The last category of money owed is called nominal bills or fictitious accounts. It serves the motive of recording any expenditure or sales incurred via a specific enterprise or dealer. All the ones money owed that have simplest been prepared in call fall below this category. Let us check a easy instance to apprehend this concept higher. If an employee gets a month-to-month salary, a manufacturing unit employee receives month-to-month wages, an agent receives a fee, and a moneylender gets an hobby, they all essentially get cash in hand. Regardless of what label it could be described under, be it commission, revenue, hobby, or wages, it all basically method coins. Cash is the only regular aspect this is not unusual to some of these monetary transactions. In the absence of those nominal heads or tags that classify the special kinds of transactions, it turns into almost not possible to apprehend what type of expenditure or sales is incurred. It becomes hard to take the necessary steps to cut down any unreasonable spending, and this may become a problem for the firm ultimately. This is why a separate account is opened for each head of expenditure or earnings, together with salaries, lease payments, commissions, discounts, hobbies, and so on. These accounts are debited whenever that is an expenditure or loss and credited if any revenue is generated.

Double-Entry Systems

When it comes to keeping financial records, there are specific structures which are extensively followed by means of maximum companies. They are the single-access structures and double-entry structures. It is the double-access gadget this is more efficient on the orderly recording of specific agencies' financial transactions in a scientific manner. When it involves recording these business transactions, this technique is most popularly used by the bulk of groups.

In this device, as the call suggests, each transaction is recorded in its twofold elements. The fundamental precept here is that every transaction has fundamental components; one element involves giving even as the alternative issue includes receiving. Whoever gets some thing in the transaction is referred to as the debtor, and whoever offers something is called the creditor.

In the double-access system, both the components of giving in addition to receiving could be recorded in phrases of the concerned money owed which are being credited or debited. The account that receives the gain is credited with the gain. For instance, on every occasion dealer A purchases a commodity from well worth $500 from dealer B on credit score, each the bills are affected on the identical time. Since goods or assets might be entering the business, the consumer's account may be debited with $500. The client's account will consequently be receiving a selected gain worth $500.

On the alternative hand, trader B's account can be credited with $500 because he may be supplying the products, and could, consequently, be rendering a gain. Similarly, if there may be a transaction regarding the change of furnishings through coins, each the bills could be affected concurrently (i.E., the furniture account and the coins account). Since the organization is purchasing furnishings, it is basically equivalent to the purchase of an asset via the business, and cash is likewise leaving the enterprise as a shape of fee for the fixtures, the coins account can be credited, whereas the fixtures account may be debited.

We can see that beneath the double-entry device, the entire quantity of all of the debit entries is constantly equal to the sum general of the credit score entries. If this isn't taking place, then it denotes that there was an errors made in the recording of transactions. You will have to go into reverse via the entries to find in which the error turned into made. For recording a business transaction in the suitable way, there are sure guidelines of double-access which you'll want to learn about with a view to keep away from these mistakes, and you will learn more about them inside the subsequent sections.

All factors of a business transaction are recorded under the double-access system of account control. Therefore, this device enables construct a complete and dependable database of all of the monetary transactions that your enterprise or groups may be involved in. The availability of dependable economic records makes it lots less difficult for the management to make proper financial decisions that are backed through strong and reliable financial information. The entries of all of the economic transactions which might be recorded within the ebook of accounts could be used to prepare monetary statements. Therefore, the double-access machine bureaucracy the backbone of basic bookkeeping.

On the alternative hand, the single-access device is a bookkeeping device that does not comply with the double-access machine and does not report the 2-fold issue of each economic transaction. Usually, best a cashbook containing the private bills are maintained under the unmarried-access device. The economic transactions are often recorded in a haphazard way, and this does not deliver a whole image of all of the financial transactions and the overall financial kingdom of the company. This machine is fairly unreliable, and because of the unsystematic way wherein monetary data is recorded, it is pretty ineffective. It is fine acceptable for small-scale organizations where the owner is for my part chargeable for the supervision of the companies' monetary affairs. Apart from this, beneath the single-access machine, monetary statements and even trial balances can't be prepared with a purpose to gauge the effectiveness and the arithmetical accuracy of the books of accounts which might be being maintained. Therefore, this method of information series is as good as vain to your commercial enterprise.

Single-Entry System

Unlike maximum principles in accounting, the single-access system of facts series does not have a clear cut or intricate definition. In reality, it is not clean to sincerely define this gadget of statistics access. The only becoming definition for this gadget of records access is that it's miles nothing however an all-faulty double-access device of records access. Moreover, this is a gadget of facts entry that is developed via certain companies to fulfill their unique needs by changing the double-access machine via a realistic method. This is why this device of records collection does no longer paintings as efficiently as the double-access device for most agencies. This machine simplest calls for the protection of the naked critical books of debts without following strict guidelines or rules that have been set in place by using the double-access device. Under this device, all the economic statements and transactions aren't considered, and most effective certain books of subsidiary data or letters are maintained, whereas the extra important ones aren't taken underneath attention while bookkeeping. So, this is why a unmarried-access system of facts collection is nothing but a double-entry device that is customized via the customers to fit the ease of the commercial enterprise proprietor. As cited in advance, the single-access machine of facts access best presents an incomplete database of financial bills. Under this machine, for positive monetary transactions, each the components of the economic transaction are recorded whereas, for different transactions, most effective one impact of the transaction is recorded. Usually, small business owners, small-scale traders, traders, small-scale pharmaceutical suppliers, or even a few attorneys generally tend to choose this approach of bookkeeping.

Rules of Debit and Credit

The double-entry system of records access data both factors of any financial transaction, i.E., both the receiving of values as well as the giving of values. These factors of a financial transaction are prominent from each other in terms of debit and credit score. An account is able to both receiving and giving economic values to external entities. When an account gets a specific benefit, the amount is debited, while if it offers benefits or values to any other entity, the quantity might be credited from the account. Since every financial enchantment will have an effect on as a minimum two different accounts, one account will acquire a advantage, while the alternative account might be imparting the aforementioned benefit. Different rules and recommendations had been framed and set in location for the ideal credit score and debit of monetary price from personal accounts, real money owed, and nominal money owed. You will study the fundamental guidelines of credit score and debit in the following section.

Personal Accounts

For non-public bills, the basic rule is that the receiver might be debited, whereas the lender may be credit. Following this rule, the account of the individual that will receive a gain is debited with the economic cost of the transaction, whereas the account of the individual imparting the gain might be the credit score. For instance, if you are purchasing goods from trader A on credit, the 2 accounts which are involved on this economic transaction are trader A's account and your purchase account. Trader A's account is also a non-public account; by using following the aforementioned rule, his account could be credited with the monetary value of the transaction in query. Likewise, considering that you'll make the fee to Trader A, your purchase account might be debited with the identical amount.

Real Accounts

The fundamental rule to follow for this account is that each one transactions that convey in revenue into the enterprise should be debited from the account, and any transactions that reason the outflow of money from your commercial enterprise will be credited from your account. If your enterprise involves purchasing inventory, then the inventory this is subsequently received is essentially coming into the enterprise account, and the stock account might be debited. Likewise, in case your business or corporation acquires furnishings in trade for cash, the furnishings account may be debited, while the cash account will be credited with the equal account.

Nominal Accounts

For nominal money owed, all expenses and losses need to be debited from the accounts, whereas all earning and sales gains have to be credited from the concerned money owed. For instance, if month-to-month wages ought to be paid to a worker, the accounts which might be concerned in these transactions are the wages account of the running and firm's cash account. Since wages preserve economic price, it's miles part of the nominal account, and the salary that is being paid to the worker can be taken into consideration to be a business fee and will, therefore, be debited from your corporation's coins account. Similarly, in case your corporation gets any commissions, dividends, or sales, then your concerned coins account could be credited with the amount in question when you consider that it is considered to be a source of earnings for your business.

You will best be capable of document all of your commercial enterprise transactions accurately in case you are retaining these kinds of basic rules in mind. As you cross emerge as greater acquainted with those regulations, you may begin learning that for economic transactions regarding exclusive bills of different sorts, applicable guidelines want to be carried out that allows you to record those transactions accurately. For example, the payment of wages or salaries affects both the revenue account of the employees as well as the coins account of the discern firm. The profits accounts of the workers are nominal debts, while the cash account of the firm is a actual account. Therefore, the latter part of the second one rule and the former part of the 0.33 rule is relevant in this situation. This approach that the simple rule on this transaction could be to debit all expenses and losses and credit score any asset or cash that goes out of the corporation. By applying this rule, the cash account could be credited, while the earnings debts will be debited with the identical amount.

The Importance of Debit and Credit

Whenever a non-public account is debited throughout any transaction, then it can essentially mean 3 various things relying upon the phrases of the financial transaction. If a brand new account is opened, if the brand new account is debited towards a specific person or even another enterprise company, then that man or woman or business will become the new debtor. If the account is a pre-existing account, and a specific debtor is debited all over again, it will replicate an boom in the debtor's obligation to the said business. If it's far a creditor's account this is debited, it reduces the debt that the commercial enterprise owes the creditor. A creditor of any business agency can even emerge as its debtor if the quantity payable to him is decreased after the debit access became posted.

Every time a personal account is credited with advantages, it implies the subsequent matters; if a new account is credited with a gain, then the man or woman to whom the account belongs will now be the creditor of the commercial enterprise.

If a pre-current account of a creditor is credited by the business, this implies that the sum this is payable to this creditor has expanded. This, in turn, increases the debt of the commercial enterprise. However, if an current debtor's account is credited, because of this the debtor's debt has elevated.

For actual debts, this will either suggest that the value of the asset is increasing or that the enterprise has controlled to collect more of a selected sort of asset. Likewise, if it's miles a actual account this is being credited, this implies that the fee of the asset this is being credited has depreciated in cost. It also can suggest that the enterprise has maximum likely disposed of the asset or as a minimum part of the asset.

Conclusion

We have blanketed the basics of bookkeeping, explaining in element the subject of bookkeeping and the basic information required for bookkeeping. The significance of bookkeeping for agencies can't be over emphasized, as we have proven throughout this e book. This e book will allow you're making clever decisions to your enterprise as you may now have increased your primary information and information of the issue matter and can proceed with self assurance.

In knowledge bookkeeping, it's miles essential to apprehend the records of bookkeeping, which began with historical investors taking inventory in their goods and transactions. They commenced from the best form of bookkeeping, which is single entry bookkeeping, and it's miles still used in lots of small companies today. The records of bookkeeping in its earliest shape changed into the idea of the superior bookkeeping methods we've these days.

The importance of bookkeeping was also analyzed in this e book. We had been capable of see the usefulness of bookkeeping for each the usage of commercial enterprise owners and investors alike. Yes, bookkeeping does help enterprise proprietors in making plans, making choices and maintaining tabs on the fitness popularity of the business. For investors and different fascinated events it continues them updated on the health of the commercial enterprise in a bid to know if their investments will turn out profitably and certainly gives them a preferred idea of the state of the enterprise. It is also useful in choice making, with an expertise of account statements and different accounting facts, which we have covered with this e book.

We have covered why the enterprise desires to have a simple hold close of accounting and bookkeeping, the variations among bookkeeping and accounting and why they are used concurrently in business. The variations among the 2 concepts make it even easier to recognize bookkeeping and accounting successfully. After analyzing this e-book, it's far expected that your knowledge of bookkeeping is improved and you've an expertise of the motive of retaining accurate books.

Keeping facts of the business involves the use of certain varieties of sheets, books and journals. Financial statements, balance sheets, income statements and many other economic documents were covered. These sheet or books have their own uses and are ways of transmitting information to each the commercial enterprise owners and the capability investors. There is some specific statistics you may be looking for that you'll find in a specific e-book or sheet, which includes the profitably of the commercial enterprise, is the commercial enterprise within the pink, cash flow, and many others.

Accounting and bookkeeping are essential in running a enterprise and are frequently used interchangeably. Knowing the difference and the significance of each will make you recognize their feature. The information of both of them can also make a high-quality impact at the organization, the price range, the board, the bookkeeper and the accountant.

Accounting formulation are another critical thing included in this e-book, and you may discover the simplest ones on Excel sheets. You can use those sheets in calculating income statements, income and loss, fees, and for the preparing of stability sheets and other economic reviews. The project is a tedious task and will require attention to get all of the figures and calculations accurate. It can require experienced and expertise to preserve the consequences errors-unfastened.

It is essential that you have basic knowledge of accounting to help prevent against being defrauded. Knowing your stock helps save you theft, or lets in you to catch theft early, earlier than it becomes a extreme a problem. Understanding your monetary statements facilitates save you you from being taken gain of via accountants, bookkeepers or managers. Understanding your commercial enterprise allows you to test your information to assist save you mistakes, inclusive of mistakes main to accelerated taxes, or unnecessary bank prices.

Accounting is one of the typical talents that may be observed in each business in every enterprise you come across. Everyone's enterprise calls for bookkeeping, regardless of their length and the kind of enterprise they're walking. Banks, engineering firms, grocery stores, thrift stores and even having a garage sale calls for a few kind accounting. Hence, maintaining accounts is very important in jogging any sort of business or authorities business enterprise.

This book exposes small enterprise owners to an knowledge of bookkeeping in order to to assist them appreciate its importance and preparation of debts. It was stated that small businesses rarely take bookkeeping critically and it has been proven that proper accounting and evaluation is certainly incredibly worthwhile for small businesses. We were capable to investigate groups that preserve up with their accounting as compared to the ones that don't take their accounting significantly. We discovered that keeping your books up to date will help you prosper on your enterprise.

Actually, you won't need to lease the offerings of professional accountants that will help you maintain your books intact as a small commercial enterprise; it's miles some thing you may examine and manage by yourself with the basics provided on this book. Learn the way to preserve the only form of bookkeeping your self and watch how your enterprise improves. As a small enterprise proprietor, you want no longer make it too complicated, as you can use the handiest form of bookkeeping in your business.

This ebook has furnished you with an area to your enterprise and may assist set you apart from your competition that won't be as astute as you. You can follow the standards found out in this e-book to your commercial enterprise and notice how a great deal of a drastic change you will revel in. It truly can help make your business a success. You can be amazed to peer that simple, correct bookkeeping can growth the amount of cash on your pocket.

www.ingramcontent.com/pod-product-compliance
Lightning Source LLC
Chambersburg PA
CBHW071235210326
41597CB00016B/2067